I0080610

Newlywed Confidential

Newlywed Confidential

REVEALING THE UNTOLD TRUTHS OF BECOMING ONE

Tamara S Williams

Copyright © 2016 Tamara S Williams
All rights reserved.

ISBN-13: 9780692718971
ISBN-10: 0692718974
Library of Congress Control Number: 2016911394
Grow Strong LLC, Breinigsville, PA

Dedication

I dedicate this book to my wonderful husband, Raymon. I am still so happy you chose me, and I am so grateful that we grew through our beginning years, learned to love deeper, and changed for the better. I love you forever and will always be your "Good Thing".

To my daughters who are completely amazing, you have made me a better woman by having you and I know there is so much in store for you both in the future. Rayna and Aria, I pray for all that God will do in and through your lives, and for the beautiful women you will become. Thank you to my wonderful and supportive parents, who taught me through their love what family and marriage look like, and for that I am forever grateful. I love you Richard and Cheryl Strong.

I also dedicate this book to every person assigned to encourage me through this process: A huge thank you to my mentors and marriage counselors Kristina Davis and Pastor Phillip Davis, we thank for all that you poured into Raymon and me. I would also like to give a special thank you to Coach Nikki Church for inspiring me when I felt like giving up and Mrs. Gladys for giving me direction when I needed it. I pray that God richly blesses Krisette Cole for editing my content with her beautiful touch; I know you are truly anointed. I also want to thank my wonderful friends Maygen, Jahanna, Janicca, Natasha, Tatanashe, Melody, Ashley, Bianca, Angel, Tioana, Tonya, Erica, Ericka, Tiffani, Nakia, Marquita, Courtney, Quinetta, Tanisha, Melanie, Alicia, Katrina, my shiloh family, and Shootworks photography. Thanks for being a part of my process.

...and to every newlywed who reads this book: I have been praying for you, and I hope you are encouraged through the pages.

Contents

Preface

Newlywed Confidential: My Metamorphosis from Ms. To Mrs.

've been there. I've been you, and I've walked through the newlywed years, and they changed me in the most beautiful ways. Sometimes change can be looked at as a negative word; however, for me, being a newlywed was a beautiful metamorphosis: going from Ms. to Mrs. In the Bible, whenever God changes someone's name, that person takes on a new purpose or responsibility, and that's what I want to describe throughout the pages of this book.

I pray that the *Newlywed Confidential* files give you an inside look at the newlywed years of marriage, which are best known as the getting-to-know-you phase of being husband and wife. It's the phase during which you grow, learn, and transition into the married life.

I thought after I had prepared, gone to counseling, and kept God at the center of everything, that it would be completely care-free and easy, right? So in 2007 when I took the walk across the bridge from singleness into marriage, I realized that I had unintentionally brought a lot of my single mind-set with me, and a lot of me needed to be transformed. It wasn't at all that I wanted to bring that mind-set with me. Frankly, I had been to so many teachings, read so many books, and attended so many "before-you-say-I-do" events that I didn't even know I still had a single mind-set! By the time I was married at the age of twenty-nine, I knew what I wanted—a companion. The trouble was that after absorbing all of those books, teachings, seminars, etc., I was still missing something. I hadn't grasped a simple yet profound truth. Marriage was going to change me inside and out and conform me to look more like Christ, and that meant more than just changing my last name.

Poured out from a transformed heart, these *Newlywed Confidential* files will give engaged couples, singles in waiting, and newlyweds a transparent inside look into my first years of marriage. This book was created to help two separate individuals understand the process of becoming one and to provide words for this process. I will explain some of the changes and transitions that take place when entering holy matrimony while also describing some of the fun and joy I experienced through those years. I will share some of the newlywed secrets I wish I grabbed hold of in my first years of marriage while giving you transitional advice from my first-hand experiences.

My goal is simple. My marriage changed me in the most beautiful ways, and I want to share all that I can with you, so that you may navigate the phases of marriage that are not so easy and that require the relinquishing of your plans. Ultimately, this is the only way that the two of you will become one. So,

If you want a friend in the transformation;
If you are ready to shift into the great ministry of marriage;
If this thing called marriage means so much to you that you are willing to embrace the awkward, exciting, joyful, fun, and sometimes emotional roller coaster called change; and

If you are ready to renew your mind to remember your vows then this is the book for you.

CONFIDENTIAL FILE 1

Licensed to Change

So the wedding day is over, and you're back from the honeymoon, enjoying your first couple of weeks together. Isn't this an awesome time? I would have to say that those first few weeks together were among the most wonderful and enjoyable times of my life. I hope you are enjoying them, too! Most newlyweds go through an extremely exciting wedding day with lots of family, friends, and vacations. And then, after the party is over, you get to adjust to your new life in love from that point forward. You have been given the license to love, and now it's time to settle into a new routine. The change that happens after those first few weeks can take many forms. Some days, it's an absolutely beautiful experience! You hold hands looking at new furniture, revel in learning sacred nuances about your spouse, and reminisce on that "newly old" season of wedding photos during spontaneous dates. But if I was being honest, there were days that for me felt like a roller coaster ride called "New Life," without a seatbelt to strap on tightly.

When experiencing change, some newlyweds have awkward feelings and emotions, and some have overwhelming feelings of fun and excitement. Whatever side of the fence your emotions fall on, I have learned it's OK to embrace these feelings, because it's in those moments you are able to learn new things about yourself and your spouse. No one's transition into marriage comes without some joyful and wonderful days, as well as some perplexing days. The encouraging thing is knowing that most newlyweds experience these emotions, and God wants you to build a strong foundation in your first stage.

We all—men and women, single and married, and especially *newlyweds*—can benefit from understanding that the way we begin has a profound impact on the quality of our marriages. So before I share with you some essential tools for transition and empower you with the license to change, allow me to tell you the background to this beautiful story and how it all began.

My Beginning

We met in picturesque Hampton, Virginia, where my husband was in the military, and I was working in the school system enjoying where my life was. My husband got out of the military after meeting me and decided to get a civilian job; he interviewed for a job in Pennsylvania and got the position. So not only was I preparing for my wedding day, I was also preparing to move states, preparing to start a new job, leaving all of my dearest friends, and packing up to leave *everything* behind and become the wife I desired and determined to be forever and ever. It seemed that the ink had barely dried on our marriage license when change began knocking on our door, but I was extremely excited to live this new life. A shift took place during which I had to transition out of my me-centered single and dating lifestyle into a lifestyle that now focused selflessly on him and on creating a family that God would be proud of.

Naturally, as a single person, I pretty much made all of my own decisions, doing whatever I wanted and coming and going as I pleased. So it was a big shift, going from being the only one involved in making all of my decisions to including another person in all of my life responsibilities. As a female who was raised to get her education and take care of herself, I needed some time to fully embrace these shifting roles. I lived a very independent lifestyle, and so did my husband. I thought that, because I saw my parents' great marriage, I understood what I was getting into, but I soon learned that my heart had not embraced some of the realities. The light bulb didn't come on for me until year two of my marriage, when I realized that the thing that was undergoing big changes was me. God had begun the process of transforming my heart in areas that I had not given him access to and were not previously touched. I was learning what love really was and how to love in a deep way.

I believe it's fair to say that, in today's culture, singles are encouraged to live their lives, get an education, and enjoy much of life before settling down with anyone. The world teaches us how to have fun and glamorizes wedding ceremonies as a goal you should accomplish, but somewhere in the midst of the wedding planning, we have lost the idea of the covenant we are stepping into. This view can leave us unprepared and unaware of the depth of transformation that we need to embrace in order to be successfully married. The newlywed journey caused me to adjust my heart to the realities of my new decision of love and embrace the fullness of this beautiful marriage covenant.

Has your metamorphosis started yet? If it has, I'm glad! If it hasn't, give it some time. Both marriage and courtship have special tools that allow you to face many areas that you need to address and may not have faced when you were alone. They force you to think differently, teach you to handle situations from new perspectives, and ultimately cause you to grow.

Even though I had committed to this new view with the stroke of a pen and a sweet vow from my lips on August 4, 2007, I didn't fully understand what it all meant. Even after attending premarital counseling sessions and obtaining a concept in my head of what the counselors meant when speaking of marriage, I hadn't fully grasped an understanding of my new position. God began to show me that he had a beautiful purpose for me in being a wife and that my husband and I would bring out the best in each other along this journey. I began to see and feel the beat of heart transformation, as I internalized fully all that I was becoming in going from Ms. to Mrs. and as a result of this love.

Initially, all I knew was that I was marrying the man of my dreams, the one I had waited for, the one whom I would grow old with, so I was filled with excitement. As a newlywed I began to see how God was going to use my marriage to help my maturity and growth as a person and that he uses marriage not only as an avenue for love but also for transformation.

Releasing My Single Tendencies

Singleness kept me in a protective force field of self, and marriage forced me into practicing more service and selflessness. The husband's affairs become the wife's and the wife's become the husband's, and together you become a better team. When my husband and I were single, we each had our own place, our own car, our own money, and our own structure. Blending our two lives became our biggest struggle, and we both dug our feet into our own way so strongly that some days, it felt like a boxing match of wills. We were so used to living on our own that both of us were struggling to give in to the other person, so in the early months, it felt like my brain was swirling trying to figure it all out. There were days I could hear God's soft whisper that I needed to release the reigns of control and to trust him and allow him to effect the change he was trying to make in me.

Have you ever seen a cocoon? Undoubtedly, it is one of the most wondrous moments of childhood when you first get the concept of exactly what happens in the cocoon, as the very simple caterpillar becomes a beautiful butterfly. Cocoons change something normal into something extraordinary. Quickly, I understood that marriage is like a cocoon. I was pushed into a cocoon of transformation—leaping from single woman to married woman—and it was not always a comfortable space. The cocoon symbolizes the transformation I was undergoing as a new wife, understanding my vulnerabilities and accepting new responsibilities. My husband and I were both releasing the ways we had functioned during our dating phase and allowing God to transform us. I didn't change overnight, and neither does a caterpillar, but my beginning years helped shape me into not only a better wife but also a better person. When a caterpillar creates a cocoon by spinning around itself and creates a hardened chrysalis, inside that chrysalis a beautiful metamorphosis is happening; the caterpillar is changing!

The first five years of marriage parallel what's happening inside of a cocoon, because it takes spins, turns, ups, and downs to create a beautiful togetherness. The cocoon protects the caterpillar from prey as it changes, so let's use the cocoon to symbolize God as the outer layer of protection for your union. Inside the cocoon disks are forming into different tissues, and once the caterpillar's process is complete, every part of the dissolved caterpillar's body has new parts formed. This is an amazing picture of what it's like to come out of your single state into your married place. A beautiful transition is happening, taking you from girlfriend to wife or boyfriend to husband and making you into all you need to be for your mate.

After leaping into marriage, I needed to become reacquainted with myself because I now had a new function. While single, I was very focused and earned two degrees; served in ministry, mentoring teens; and spent lots of time with friends doing my own thing. Now, I had to embrace and understand how my priorities would shift. I had to begin to see my priorities with different eyes and know that my new priorities were gifts from God and had significant purpose. I had to get honest and realize that priorities change when you say "I do," and that doesn't lessen your impact; it just makes it more strategic and specific.

When you're dating, you get to soak up thinking about just yourself, because that's what dating allows you to do. Then the mind-set shift happens within marriage, and now you have to think of someone else before yourself. The man now has to put on his role as priest of the home, provider, and protector, which is totally different from being responsible for only himself. He is now responsible for an entire family, which entails family discussions, big decisions, and an awareness of how the family structure is developing. As a newlywed, single tendencies are still transforming and falling off of you, and the greatest comfort in all of that is knowing that it's *normal*!

No one jumps into marriage and begins to operate like someone who has been married for twenty years. Be aware of how you have progressed, encourage yourself in the places where you have made sacrifices, and applaud your process. Letting go of my single tendencies was something God highlighted to me, and I had to allow him to change some of my perspectives. Being a newlywed involves a variety of emotions, but the great thing is that God knows we are experiencing them and is walking with us through them. God cares about every detail of every season of our marriages, so never neglect to talk to God about every thought or emotion along the way. Use wise married couples who can help you navigate through the transition, and always remember to talk to God about it.

Many people don't like to talk about the feelings that can be associated with transition, because they can be very vulnerable ranging from cloud nine, a soft ocean breeze, or even a roller coaster. I remember the days when I thought, "Wow, those wedding vows are real, because I now have to put them into practice." I vowed that I would love for better or worse, but I wasn't really thinking we would have any "worse" moments, because why wouldn't they all be "better"? The world teaches that love should be free from turbulences of any kind, and that makes your marriage successful, right? You find the love of your life and enjoy perfection forever. But perfection wouldn't be the best word to describe the marriage journey; growth together would a better way of viewing it. Love looks like laying your life down for another person's well-being and betterment and loving that person with a sacrificial love.

Transition Time

As a single, I was not wise enough to understand or listen to the advice of older married couples who were trying to enlighten me about this journey. So let me advise you to try to heed their words and have a teachable spirit as they share their experiences. I will admit I was pretty prideful in thinking that my story would never be anything like those of the other married couples I saw around me. I thought my marriage was exempt from any trials because we were perfect for each other; why would anything be uncomfortable? I never thought we needed to transition and learn, because didn't we do that while we were dating? It never dawned on me that I would need a transition time as a newlywed, and I believe that *transition* is the best word to describe the changes that take place in the first years. The transition is the process or period of changing from one state or condition to another; it's a movement, development, or evolution from one form to another. The description I used in my earlier analogy about the caterpillar in its cocoon describes the beautiful metamorphosis that transpires during this transition. Just think—If you were able to look inside of a cocoon, the transformation you would probably see would be an oozing chrysalis or a soupy mess that might spill out; however, inside that chrysalis are a group of highly organized cells that are developing inside the egg. The caterpillar needs the mess so that it can mature into a butterfly or moth, so while your union is in the cocoon stage, you may have a couple of messy moments, but know it's moving toward the beautiful place.

When experiencing change, you may feel like you want to escape the cocoon's cramped spaces before all of the rapid cell division is complete. But you cannot escape because the changes that you go through give you the wisdom to give to those marriages coming behind yours. Don't be afraid of the change, and don't be frightened of uncomfortable discussions while learning about each other as husband and wife. It's very normal to experience extreme satisfaction as well as growing pains. The pains always lead you to a better, more settled, and deeper place. Your love can be firmly rooted and substantiated in the truth of love and not just the concept of true love.

The transition is often just like a little sandpaper rounding out the rough edges of your relationship, and usually, it's all a part of the process. Yes, I will admit I came into marriage like a little school girl, bright eyed and bushy tailed, thinking nothing could ever be too challenging, especially if my husband and I had the same beliefs. Little did I know how God would use my marriage for his glory and write a more beautiful love story then I could have imagined for myself. All the transitions we went through together formed me into a more purified version of myself and made me into the best mate for my husband.

I do is the beginning

The day you say "I do" is legally the day you unite as one, but it takes time to display that oneness. Please again let me be the one to scream and say that *it is OK* for it to take time! I remember the day I realized I didn't have to have it all figured out. I needed to have a willing heart and to soak up all that I was learning. God took two previously self-focused singles, put them together, and then began to purify their love. During this process of change, I didn't get it right every day, nor do I get it right every day now. However, I let go of the perfection complex and just embraced the art of becoming, by intentionally cultivating my marriage.

The day I got married, I just knew that my husband had gotten the best woman in the world—the one whom God had designed just for him. I had prepared, prayed, dated, and gotten the family's approval and now? Now he got me! I was so excited to have a life with my new husband that nothing else in the world mattered to me. He had chosen me over all the others, and I set my mind to make the transition from being the best girlfriend to being the best wife just for him. At that point, I knew I was willing to love him through anything that came our way, and I was very vocal about how I felt about my knight in shining armor. The vows were becoming real, and I could clearly see that the process of becoming one would take more than just a moment at the altar. So I began to ponder the process and search for solutions. What I found forced me to be real with myself.

As I dug into my study, it became clear to me that I had misunderstood this word, *become.* Because of the prenuptial preparation that I had put in, I thought that I had already become. In reality, *to become* means to undergo a change or development. To be made suitable for.

Honestly, after reading that definition I thought "Why would either of us have to change if we specifically chose each other?" I knew that I couldn't change my personality or the things that made me uniquely myself, but what I didn't realize was that marriage would compel me to grow and change in areas that I had kept hidden in my single state. God used my marriage to cause me to address certain areas of my life that were really not highlighted when I was by myself. I seemed to think I was a pretty good catch! I was goal oriented, I loved my family, and I enjoyed quality time with my man. An all-around first-class type of girl. However, it was the inaugural year of our marriage that began to tear down these walls of self-perception. That first year initiated a process of becoming one with my new husband. It was the year that thrust me head first into the beginning of a new level of understanding. It transformed my sweetly simplistic thoughts of marriage and transformed my thoughts into a higher and more mature thought pattern. . That place beyond the vow, where love is uncovered and everything gets real.

Words for the process

Are you OK with the process of becoming? Are you OK with the thought that everything is melting together gradually? Yes, you had a ceremony declaring your oneness, but that oneness has just started forming! When thinking of oneness, the word *fusion* came to mind, so I investigated fusion welding. Fusion welding is the process used in metalworking to join two pieces of metal. Before the two pieces of metal come together, the surfaces of the pieces have to be shaped and cleaned, to ensure the strongest weld possible. Preparation of the surfaces before joining is critical to ensuring the integrity of the joint piece. The fusion process requires high-temperature phases in order to meld two separate things together.

I don't think that I need to tell you that the word *fusion* has ended up being a great word when talking about becoming one and walking through some of the newlywed phases. I believe that you are already nodding your head in agreement. When fusing things together, there are high-temperature moments and low-temperature moments, and those moments can be interpreted as part of the merging process rather than breakdowns. They happen because when any object is undergoing change, the object requires some high temperatures and is placed in some uncomfortable spaces in order to transform.

Don't be afraid of the high-temperature days and think that something is wrong when uncomfortable situations arise; it's just part of the transformation process. I remember feeling so fearful when I had high-temperature moments in my marriage because I always thought that something must be wrong with us, when in actuality we were just changing.

When I was changing from girlfriend to wife there were many times I thought that if we were disagreeing then that meant we were headed to divorce court or that I had made the wrong decision in choosing a mate. That couldn't have been further from the truth. The truth was that most marriages have this figuring-you-out phase that can only take place within confines of the marriage. So whether you're in a high-fusion moment or low-fusion moment, don't fear the temperatures because they will fluctuate according to the season you're in. Those fluctuations will meld your heart to your mate's heart because you've had to work through them and learn to love each other when it wasn't easy; you are really experiencing what it means to be one. Learn from every temperature in your beginning years, and write down your lessons because you will need to pass them on to help the next newlywed couple through their newlywed chronicles.

Marriage is fun and enjoyable journey of two people who have fallen in love, but it is also designed to display to the world how God loves us and to conform us to love the way he loves. So enjoy the transformation process! Whether you believe it or not, every couple gets the opportunity to go through these transitions, and I hope when reading this, you see the beautiful metamorphosis. Every great team takes time to develop teamwork, so I encourage you to grow and see the beauty of the process of your becoming one, because you will look back and see how far you have come and how much more is still to come.

The Transition Triangle Δ

(God, New Husband, New Wife)

1. What single tendency did you bring with you into marriage that you now have to surrender or be more aware of daily?

2. Study question: As a new husband or new wife, what does "submit to one another" mean to you?

3. Learn, Embrace, and Transform- What are you learning? What are you embracing? And what is Transforming?

4. How can you rid yourself of the perfection complex?

   Meditation: Scripture focus: Romans 8:29- For God knew his people in advance, and chose them to become like his Son, so that his Son would be the firstborn among many brothers and sisters.

Write good changes that have happened in your life so far, as a result of being in this relationship?

_____

_____

Prayer for the Transitioning Spouse

Lord, thank you for the gift of marriage. I thank you that as you have given me this as a gift. Though I am still growing into the responsibility you have given me, I pray that as I grow, you continue to bless our union as we grow together. Lord, you said in your word, behold you make all things new, so help me Lord to transition into my new life with grace and love. Help me to be the spouse you desire me to be for the mate you have given me. Thank you for teaching me how to be more like you and conforming me more into your likeness. I am grateful for the exciting future we have to together and blessed to understand a deep love. In my own strength Lord, I don't know everything it takes to be a wife or a husband, but you knew I was equipped to handle it. Teach me every beautiful aspect of marriage. Take my old single habits, mind-sets, independence, selfishness, and self-protective ways, and make me patient, kind, good, faithful, gentle, and self-controlled. Make us a team, not pursuing separate, competitive, or independent lives, but working together, overlooking each other's faults and weaknesses for the greater good of the marriage. Make me a new person, Lord. Give me a fresh perspective, and help me to see through my partner's eyes. I thank you Lord for giving me wisdom through my transition and grace to be a newlywed.

CONFIDENTIAL FILE 2

It's Brand New

The fun part of the first few years of marriage is creating a new flow. After you say "I do" and you have met the love you always waited for, you ride away full of the hopes and dreams bubbling in your heart and excited about one of your dreams becoming a reality. What's great about this spot is it's all new: a blank canvas ready to get the first few strokes of the paintbrush. No matter what you knew previously or saw from your family growing up, you now have the opportunity to create a new family dynamic with new memories. It is so much fun creating new memories together and establishing your family legacy.

Use these precious moments to discover the uniqueness of your marriage dynamic and make critical choices that will shape many generations to come. It is a fantastic time of looking ahead to the future and all that God has planned for your new life together. Intentionally use this opportunity to reflect, ask each other even more about your own family histories, and discuss the impact that the decisions that you are making together now will have in the future of your generational line.

So, what family dynamics did you bring to the table? My husband and I brought unique family dynamics to the table. One of us grew up in a traditional two-parent home, and the other was raised by a single parent. It was an interesting paradox. These vastly different environments shaped each of us into the person whom the other now loved deeply. However, dating had made us slightly oblivious to the potential challenges that our family differences would pose in our blending together as a unit. So, through moments of flourishing and faltering, it became apparent that we would need to bring a third party into our discussions. Someone to help us take those nuances that made us individually unique and to combine them in a beautiful way to make our union an immaculate work of art and not merely splattered paint on the page. So we made a wise choice and decided to turn to counseling.

Our counselors went right to work helping us merge our two different life experiences. During one session, a counselor asked us what we valued about each other's families. What a big issue—what an incredible moment! Acknowledging the great things about each other's upbringing allowed us to reflect on the importance of not only our individual experiences but also the experiences that shaped us as individuals. It presented us with the opportunity to strip our minds of the thoughts that were actually holding us back in our marriage—thoughts that our own upbringing was the best and only way. Realizing that each of our upbringings had produced this person whom we now loved brought great clarity. We were given a golden opportunity to understand each other's perspectives. Once our minds were set on that, we were empowered to begin learning how to pull great things from each of our backgrounds, determine what fit into our current family dynamic, and decide which things were best left in the past. It brought the freedom to imagine and dream together for our own family and relinquish a silent competition about whose ways were best.

A good example of this was when I tried to compare my father's lifestyle to my husband's lifestyle. I was raised by a man from Mississippi who loves yard work and sports. I married a man who was born in the South but raised on the West Coast. He enjoys travel and adventure. Even though I knew of their differences, I expected that my husband would operate similarly to my father. I had already learned to be grateful for the qualities that my father modeled for me, but I was still learning to be grateful for the ways that my husband would demonstrate those same qualities. Let me tell you—it's never a good idea to make blanket comparisons in marriage. Though my husband emulates noble qualities like my father (such as humility), I had to learn to allow my husband to be himself. Once I discovered this, I began an incredible journey to embrace and rejoice in seeing my husband live authentically with joy as the man God created him to be. The virtue is what is to be savored, not pigeonholing our spouses into an explicit demonstration.

Understanding each other's backgrounds helped us to see through the eyes of the other person, to consider how they grew up and what their top priorities were in life. Marriage provides a unique opportunity to see through the eyes of someone else and teaches you to embrace each other's differences as your family unit develops. Like many, the two of you have brought completely different backgrounds together, and that can be quite easy or quite challenging. Truly, we could spend chapters on this topic, simply

TAMARA S WILLIAMS

because it hits so close to home for all newlyweds. So as you continue to learn to embrace each other's differences it makes great opportunities for building a solid foundation.

No matter how much you prepare during the dating process, there is still a metamorphosis that happens between the two of you as your marriage develops. Many of our expectations and ideals blend together, and we had the opportunity to grow together as individuals. My husband used to tell me on every anniversary, "We are still growing," and when he said it, it would aggravate me. I thought "Still growing? Shouldn't we have gotten this before marriage?" The answer, I found out, was *no*. It isn't possible to learn and understand every aspect of ourselves before the wedding. Marriage involves a lot of on-the-job training. Patience is needed, not all transitions are instantaneous, and just because you hold the same values and beliefs doesn't mean you don't have a process to work out together.

Managing New High Expectations

I walked into my marriage with an enormous pile of expectations that I am sure even Superman could not have achieved. I had this picture of how I thought everything was going to flow, never embracing the idea of the development process that has to happen when going from dating to marriage. Sometimes because we have great dating experiences, we get frustrated when marriage is not everything we ever envisioned immediately following the ceremony. I realized that the new flow in my home had to be developed and not copied from something I saw in a movie or in someone else's relationship. I reacted poorly to the transitions and the adjustments at the beginning of marriage, which often made me believe that I had failed or made a mistake.

One extremely challenging night during our first year, I remember lying on the bed, thinking, "Did we make a mistake? This is too hard!" It was that night that God started to share with me the fact that I had poor thinking and thinking that my marriage was a mistake was not the answer. Clearly, we had heard him regarding choosing each other and loved each other very much. Clearly it was not a mistake. So what was this uncomfortable sensation that I was experiencing? Why did it appear to feel difficult when it should have been easy? Just what was this struggle about? So I began to question the scripture "He who finds a wife finds a good thing." I thought, "Aren't I already good?" He would not have chosen me if I wasn't already great, right?"

I had gotten into the horrible habit of looking at the relationships of others who were not in the same place that I was and believing that my marriage was failing. Believing that I was failing. But it was not so. Through prayer and meditation on the word of God, our gracious Father helped me to realize that He was indeed changing me from my single state into a beautifully sculpted wife, made with intentionality just for my husband. And that, in this process of dying to myself, I was glorifying him.

I soon learned that I needed to give my marriage and myself time to grow, extending grace to myself to make mistakes and learn in marriage while we were creating a strong foundation. Marriage takes on the look of Jesus's love for us, which is an entirely, completely, sacrificial, all-in-all, and passionate love. So when learning to manage those high expectations in the beginning years, trust him to bring every expectation into appropriate alignment while still believing, working hard, and expecting great things in your relationship.

Adjusting Your Friendships to Your New Marriage

So this section is a tricky one because most everyone has male and female friendships before they get married. Perhaps before marriage you were more secluded and prone to be alone. Others may have had a close-knit unit of friendships leading up to their wedding days.

Regardless of what happened before the vows, you have to give yourself, your spouse, and your friendships a chance to adjust to the dynamics of your new life. It's easy to want to jump back into your friendships the way that they used to be, but it's always good (and right) to give yourself some time to adjust to your marital relationship first, and then adjust your peer friendships. I will say *do not* throw your friendships out of the window after you say "I do," because you will all need one another at different moments in your life. You may need a time of adjustment at the beginning of your marriage, when you may not talk to your close friends as you grow into your new roles and responsibilities. Be mindful of extending grace to yourself and others while you are adjusting. Friendships are essential for life and growth and are necessary in times of need. You will always have to balance your friendships and your spouse, so start with your relational priorities clearly in order.

On the other hand, associations with the opposite gender should only be maintained if the spouse is comfortable with the relationship and believes that person is trustworthy. That friend must be respectful of your marital relationship and not desire to disrupt your time with your spouse. This category of friendships should be treated very carefully. Never use friends of the opposite gender to unload all your issues on. This makes your marriage very vulnerable, creates unwanted insecurities, and leads to mistrust. I will say that you should never have an opposite-gender friendship, however, if that friendship is causing challenges within the marriage. If this is the case, reduce or cut off communication. Let's not be naive about the effects of opposite-sex friendships on marriages, especially if your spouse is not trusting of the relationship. Make sure you leave no gate open for your spouse to loose trust.

Learning to Divide Your Time

After surveying newlyweds, I realized that there was another hot topic of adjustment worth discussion. And that was the change in how you use your personal time. Some people encounter challenges with sharing time because they are used to doing things on their own. Before marriage, you spend your time primarily on what you prefer. When you sleep, when you find time for sports, hobbies, etc., is completely up to you. So the idea of sharing your time with another person (yes, even your beloved), can potentially be tricky waters to navigate. Clearly, I am not in any way saying that you cannot have your own personal time. But remember, in marriage we regard each other in all things. That means our time as well.

What if prior to marriage you were used to spending time every Saturday morning going to the salon and socializing for three hours? What if prior to marriage you went to the gym for five hours to get in a workout, and now that has to be cut down a little bit? What if you are used to having an hour of downtime right after work, and now you may have to cut that time down? I remember my first argument in marriage was over sleeping patterns, as my husband is a quiet sleeper and I like white noise. Wow, I never thought that a sleeping pattern could even create a discussion point! That was an area in which I had to extend grace to my husband while we were transitioning into oneness. The wrong thing to do would have been to disregard his needs and believe my way was the best. So take inventory and see what activities you can keep doing and which ones need to change.

It's important to know that your activities will fluctuate depending on the season. In one season, you may be busy doing lots of things together, and in another season, you may have other outside responsibilities. Be open, pray, and prioritize your life so you will know what is important in each season of life, as it will help you divide your time well.

New Unexpected Moments

Leave room in your first year for those unexpected things you didn't notice before marriage, and know that the unexpected things will cause you to grow stronger and learn about your mate in a variety of situations. I know all of us would like to believe we are fully aware our significant others on the day that we say, "I do," but we don't know our mates perfectly in the beginning. When I mention unexpected things, I mean the things you may see more of within marriage than you saw before the wedding.

You will see more of your mate's personal idiosyncrasies and be challenged to learn how to handle them. It could be financial stress, personal opinions, health crises, work difficulties, or many other things that could expose sides that you have never had to endure before. It will cause you to be more aware and more prayerful because you could be the voice that they need to hear at that moment. I remember my father telling me that sometimes things come that you didn't quite see before marriage that test your ability to trust God to guide and protect your union. I don't believe you're ever going to see every nuance in your spouse before marriage because then there would be no room for improvement, no room for growth, and no room to walk out the vows you took. There are many reasons that God put the two of you together. One of those reasons is that you're the one person assigned the task of helping your spouse become all that they were to created to become. You are the one! That's why you saw each other at the right moment in time. It was God's destiny for you to help bring out the best in each other.

You will experience at least one unexpected attribute of your partner that you didn't see during your dating period. Every newly married couple does, so there is no need to be scared or surprised when it happens. It's your moment to act and seize the opportunity to take a leap of faith that together you can work through anything. Occasionally, however, an opportunity will present itself before the "I dos" are said. I remember during my engagement, I got very sick and that sickness offered the opportunity for us to see how we would handle a situation we were not accustomed to.

Needless to say it, was very difficult for him to see me in that state of sickness and trying to comfort me during a very sensitive time of transition in our lives was hard. At that point we considered calling it quits, because I expected him to be Superman, and he expected me to be She-Ra during my illness. Never did we believe that this moment was a time of learning and growing in love. So I called my premarital counselor, told them the situation, and they asked me this pivotal question: "Can you love him even though he still learning how to handle this type of situation?" I was shocked. Why was I the one who was being asked to do this? I was frustrated that my fiancé wasn't performing the way that I desperately wanted him to under pressure. The challenge was so foreign to me—I was being asked to love him even though he was still *learning*? I thought, "If he is the one for me, then he should know! Shouldn't married life look like what my perception of marriage was once I found "the one?" I came to realize that he was in the learning process, too, and I had to embrace the fact that he had to learn how to be a husband just as I had to get to be a wife. This learning curve pertained to all circumstances, not just the perfect ones.

Marriage teaches you what God's love looks and feels like, and it shows you how to put into action the words you spoke on your wedding day. Even though some unexpected moments and situations will arise, know that God has given you the grace to walk through them. Prayer is the key to unlocking unconditional love for your new spouse and communicating with God, who created marriage. He will help you handle every situation together as you transition and explore a new life together.

New Assignment!

When you cross over into marriage, you have taken on a new role, so now your assignment has shifted, and you have a new focus. Your priorities will change. The scripture tells you that now your priority is what will please your husband and his is what will please his wife. That doesn't take away who you are as an individual. However, it does push you to think in ways you haven't thought before. You may or may not have children right now, but even when you do, that doesn't change a simple fact. Your spouse is the greatest and first assignment that God has given you, and you are to steward that assignment wisely.

Having an assignment is being given a particular duty or job in a situation. A great synonym for *assignment* is the word *commission*. When given a commission, you have been charged with a specific function and granted the power and authority to operate in a particular area. You have been commanded to love unto death. What a powerful assignment! When I think about the word *commission*, I reflect on those who are in the military and are given the command to serve in a particular branch and the awesome responsibility to serve and protect our country at the potential cost of their lives. When you got married, you were entrusted with a commission: a specific task to fulfill through your marriage. At the altar on your wedding day, you were given new orders. Those new roles gave you a promotion to a new place, new phase, increased prayer, increased sacrifice, and increased love. What a unique gift you have been given— this assignment to display what love is supposed to look like to the world through marriage. This new assignment holds new earthly responsibilities, which are not all easy to adjust to but are hugely significant nonetheless. Grab hold of the assignment, and know that if you were given the task for this season of your life, there is something that needs to be done on Earth through your union. Believe that there is purpose in your marriage and what God has joined together no man can tear it apart. You've been commissioned!

Communication with Your New Marriage Mentor

It is essential that you have a trusted marriage mentor to talk to on the days that you just don't know what to do, one who will communicate things you may be desperately needing to know as you transition through. I call these people crisis confidants—the wise men and women you are not afraid to discuss the crisis with and who will keep your information confidential.

Let's be real for a moment. Every emotion you feel while adjusting does not need to be expressed to your spouse because some situations can be gender specific, and at times it might be better to talk to a trusted mentor. I know people tell you to keep others out of your marriage, which is partially true; however, don't let disagreements go on too long without coming to some resolve about them. You cannot carry conflicts too long, or you might be dragging a record of things into years two, three, and four of your marriage. That can pose problems if these issues aren't handled and are swept under the rug for too long, and you start to smell the stench from underneath the carpet. Then you lift up the carpet, take a whiff, and wonder "How did we get here?"

You get there by avoiding conflict and not getting help to deal with the record of wrong you might be carrying. This is the beauty of marriage mentors. They've been there, they've done that, they've had their carpet cleaned and can help you to avoid the same pitfalls that made life messy for them.

When my husband and I finally went to counseling in year seven, we were bringing up things from years one and two of our marriage, because we never properly dealt with these things early on. Wise counsel was necessary to untangle some of those areas that had been left to fester for far too long, and having wise counsel doesn't mean taking your issues to your crazy friends who do not fully understand the concept of marriage and expecting them to give you great advice. I want you to reject the idea that going to counseling means you're headed to divorce court. Who gave us those ideas? Who gave us the fear that seeking outside opinions mean you can't handle marriage? Who tells you to turn and walk away at the first sign of resistance? The unwise. And this type of counsel couldn't be further from the truth. Ask God, and seek out the right mentors for both of you so that your marriage can flourish, not flop.

Establish your mentors early, because it is always good to have a third eye who can help both parties come to a solution. Don't be afraid to ask, because marriage mentors are good and actually very biblical as described in Titus 2 and other passages of scripture. This means in the beginning, you don't have it all figured out, which means you must remain humbly teachable yet protective. I will never tell you to bash your spouse with your words to anyone, but I will say this—don't be afraid to talk to someone who will lead you to the truth, because it has helped me on many occasions and preserved what the Lord desired instead of feeding into my own fleshly desires.

Discovering Your New Marriage Flavor

Is your married flavor hot sauce, cinnamon, vanilla, or maybe even a fresh herb concoction? I love talking about flavors because everyone has different taste buds. What I like to eat may not be what others like the taste of, and if you have a foodie in your life, flavor is everything. Some couples have a feeling of fun, some have a flavor of adventure, some have a flavor of travel, some have a characteristic of meaningful family interaction, some have a flavor of humanitarian service, some have a taste of athletics, some savor entertainment, who knows what your flavor may be! What I do know is yours is unique, so have fun exploring and developing what makes your marriage tick and gives it spice. There is nothing wrong with admiring other marriages for the work those husbands and wives have put in, but after you have applauded others' prosperous marriages, begin to explore your own, and make it prosperous, too. No two couples are the same, and no two relationships will ever function in the same way. When I look at my parents' relationship, their two personalities create a dynamic that cannot be replicated, but some principles can be implemented. It's so refreshing to see different dynamics in other marriages, because I love seeing the different flavors in couples. Put your one-of-a-kind stamp on your marriage legacy, and be determined to leave a powerful message. Marriage is a beautiful gift from above. It's all new, so enjoy every moment of its newness and explore, discuss, and develop your beautiful love story.

The Transition Triangle Δ

(God, New Husband, New Wife)

1. What new traditions can you implement in your new family? Start to think of those things and write them down.

2. What did your new spouse's side of the family bring to the table that is valuable?

3. Are your expectations realistic? Have you given your spouse time to grow in certain areas of their life?

4. Do you have wise, godly marriage mentors whom both you and your spouse value to talk you through the transition moments? If so, name them.

5. What gives your marriage its unique flavor?

6. Write out a marriage vision and pray over it.

Meditation Scripture: 1 Corinthians 13:4-7Love is patient, Love is Kind. It does not envy, it does not boast, it is not proud. It does not dishonor others, it is not self-seeking it is not easily angered, it keeps no record or wrongs.

Every married couple learns how to love through this scripture.

Lessons When Becoming One

Becoming One by Preferring the Other

n the beginning, you will have a lot of funny stories about the differences between you and your spouse. One person may keep the ketchup in the pantry, while the other likes the ketchup in the refrigerator. One person may like the clothes folded a certain way, and the other person doesn't care. It may even be that one person is a night owl, and the other is an early bird. The funniest stories will arise during your first years, so stay flexible and teachable because there is so much more fun left to have. The process of becoming one is learning how to prefer the other before yourself, and for some of us, that is not always an easy concept to internalize. There were still parts of my mind from my single state that believed getting married was all about what I wanted, rather than what I was giving. As you transition into marriage, naturally sometimes you think things should be done your way, and you will probably think your way is the best way. You will be challenged to learn your spouse's background and upbringing and learn to prefer the other person before yourself in some situations that arise. You are gaining another set of eyes through marriage, and through those eyes you will begin to see things from another perspective. It wasn't always easy for me when I had to prefer my spouse because I felt the emotion of weakness. I battled through what my head knew was right for our marriage and what my flesh wanted. I came to learn that, when I preferred my spouse over myself when I didn't feel like it, God was pleased with me, and we grew stronger and learned another aspect of love. I learned that love is not about what I was getting; rather, love was clearly about the moments that I chose to prefer my spouse and how it affected our togetherness. Many times, your emotions will tell you that you looked weak in a particular moment or that it was not fair that you had to prefer your spouse in a situation, but you never know how your preference may have impacted your spouse's heart in ways you never dreamed.

Becoming one is living a selfless life, a life focused more on oneness, learning to compromise, and seeing another's needs before your own. Then with one day, a vow, and a license, you now need to change your process of thinking. That process involves considering how another person feels, respecting their opinions, and coming to a decision as a team. Becoming one and preferring the other allows us to have mirror moments, and those mirror moments showed me how I had brought my single mind-set into the marriage. I remember one morning I woke with so much on my heart, crying out to God about why certain things were not going as I had imagined. Then a very special sister shared a message with me about the very scripture I had been studying. Philippians 2:3—"Do nothing out of selfish ambition or vain conceit, rather in humility value others above yourself." So I repeated that scripture over and over, thinking if I repeated this phrase enough times, I would see it in my actions. Then an "Aha!" moment came, and I realized that it was not just a cute phrase to say to get through a bad moment during marriage. Preferring someone was what I needed to implement so that a transformation could take place. Daily, I had to choose to live my life in service to my mate without expecting him to give me something in return. So after my "Aha!" moment, I thought, "How could I do this?" I was challenged with the concept that sometimes his needs may go before my own and vice versa.

I had to shift my thinking away from the self-service that courtship can sometimes cultivate. In some respects, dating is an evaluation period, seeing whether that person will cross their *T*'s and dot their *I*'s, and it's sort of a "What can you do for me?" phase. In marriage that thought pattern just doesn't work, so an adjustment in your thoughts has to take place. No one tells you when you cross over into married land that you need to switch gears from "serve me" to "service." Service is a great thing, because you are looking out for the needs of another person, and it's exactly the characteristic we all need to develop. In order to help your mind focus on that principle, I will share a scripture that I meditated on, so I could internalize the concept of serving my spouse. Matt 20:28 says "For even the Son of Man came not to be served but to serve others and to give his life as a ransom for many." Jesus came not so that we could serve him, but to save and serve all of humanity; what a great example to follow a model of service to our spouse and our family.

I had a long list of things I wanted my husband to do better, but it wasn't until I made the decision to work on myself that things began to change. Embracing a new thought pattern as a newlywed means loving without conditions, which moves you to a beautiful picture of the way God loves. Your heart learns how to truly love another person without always looking to get something in return, and this type of love opens up the doors of communication with your partner. It's a great idea to discuss ways that both of you can serve each other better and experience joy and true fulfillment. I learned this lesson the hard way after replaying and repeating my needs over and over in my head and wanting things my own way. I had many discussions about my needs, and while some of them were significant, those desires ended up backfiring because I would obsess over what my spouse was not doing, and what I was not getting. All I was seeing were the faults of my mate, and I can tell you that if you keep thinking that way too long, you will allow bitterness, resentment, and discontentment to take root in your heart. Once bitterness takes root, it becomes very hard to receive any gesture your spouse attempts, even when they try to love you. So I challenge you to SHUSH: Serve Him/Her until Something Happens. Serve when you feel like it, and when you don't, knowing that your service in love may be the action that speaks loudly and allows your love to grow.

In marriage we all have to allow God to change us first and then trust that he will reveal change to our spouses. That doesn't mean never having healthy conversations about the dynamics of your relationship. It means being patient enough to wait for some of the changes. The waiting is not always the easy part, and it takes a lot of humility, patience, and dependence on God. So I began to focus on my own metamorphosis as a wife and allow the Lord to begin his perfecting work in me. I had to stop pressing the replay button of my needs obsessively. I am not in any way disregarding personal relationship *needs* in the marital relationship, because we all have them; what I am saying is that there will be seasons and moments when you will have to prefer your spouse's needs over your own for the benefit of the marriage union.

I would advise couples to study their spouses' love languages and to read the book *Five Love Languages* by Gary Chapman, which discusses the primary needs of your spouse. It helps you to understand each other more clearly, and it teaches you to learn the way your spouse says "I love you." As you learn to prefer your mate more, your heart will take on a totally different posture. Through that posture you will be honoring God and pleasing your spouse. What a package deal! I challenge you to observe and try weekly to meet your spouse's love need.

Becoming One by Releasing Self-Centeredness

As you observe people who are getting married now, you'll notice that many people are not getting married right out of college anymore. No longer are people marrying at eighteen, nineteen, twenty, or even twenty-four. Men *and* women are waiting to get married later on in life to complete their single season. Waiting is not a bad thing at all; it just means that people who have been single for longer may need more help with the transition into marriage. I also noticed that our culture leans toward self-centeredness, and sometimes we can be oblivious to some of the self-centered tendencies we present. I struggled with self-centeredness early in my marriage because I had spent so much of my twenties alone. When I got married, I had my own things. I owned my car and my home, and so did my husband, so blending was very challenging. We had to bring our two lives together, and we were both holding on to our own ways for dear life. We came into marriage with the attitudes of independence and self-sufficiency that we were very attracted to when we were dating. The power couple, right? We loved the fact that we could both handle our business independently, but when we fell in love with each other, God knew we would change each other's lives to see things in different ways. We enjoyed spending time together dating and then going back to our own spaces—boy did we have fun! We enjoyed love, he was smart, we were serving God together, he had a great career, and so did I.

After our wonderful dates, we would go back to our own homes and dream of each other and the day that we would come together as one. Through our dating we had the opportunity to feel companionship and still not have to release any of our self-centeredness. So God took two me-centered people, put them together and taught them to prefer the other before themselves. Some days I would think we did our dating process perfectly, meaning we both loved Jesus, we prayed, we fasted, we asked my friends and family, and we loved each other, so there should be perfection, right? In our perfect social networking world where everyone posts about how magnificent their lives in marriage are, I was wondering: Was

I the only one having some adjustment difficulties? My marriage was not in a terrible place in the first years; I just mentally had the expectation that I would never have any thoughts other than "I am so in love." I never would have thought that God would use my marriage to make me look and act more like Jesus. Whoa! What a thought! That God uses our marriages to conform us and to make us better and not only for companionship.

The newlywed phase of marriage is like a blank canvas that you get to paint on every day. After embracing some scriptures on marriage, I was able to add a new color to our newlywed portrait, painting and growing closer to my husband. The Bible is a framework to help us, teach us, and instruct us to walk in love in really practical situations. My initial problem was that I often would get distracted from what God was telling me to do in my marriage and compare my relationships to others. I thought there was some perfect rubric or framework to married life. I thought, "Maybe we're weird. Is no one else experiencing transitional issues, or is no one talking about it?" I did figure out that many people don't like to talk while they are going through certain things, so they also resort to handling it alone. This is why I wanted to write this book, so that newlyweds wouldn't have to feel alone while they were still learning. I had many high expectations for my new husband, and the truth was that my spouse needed to learn to be the best husband for me, and I needed to learn to be the best wife for him. I learned that it was OK not to be super wife in the beginning, and that it was OK to transition into wifey life. The day I walked down the aisle and entered into married life did not make my new husband and I one in every aspect of our lives. It takes time to learn to be a good wife or husband for your spouse, and I wanted to write about this to assure you that oneness will happen. You will look at your spouse in amazement of all that you were able to overcome together. The learning process is like making the perfect dish; you keep adding seasoning until it tastes just right.

Becoming One by Delighting in Differences

So, yes, my hubby and I are opposites: the classic opposites-attract story. Then add the visible male versus female differences and that takes you to Learning Curve Avenue on the journey called newly-wed life. I am a very free-spirited person, and my husband, is the more detail-oriented one. Needless to say, my free nature was a thorn in my husband's flesh some days, and at times his structure made me feel like I was just all over the place. It took us a couple of years to learn that our own methods were not always the best, but we were bringing together the ways in which we complimented each other. In our single state, we are used to doing things the way we have always done them and not really having to change our modes of operation. I eventually I listened to my spouse's need for structure, and he listened to my need for more flexibility, and we attempted to meet each other in the middle.

We quickly came to see that, within our marriage, our modes of operation, thoughts, emotions, and processes were different and purposely designed as such. At one point as newlyweds, our differences seemed to be highlighted, which caused tension, but over time we have learned that our uniqueness brought out the best in us both. During our first years of marriage, our differences seemed to be magnified, and all we could see were the faults in each other, but the beauty of God's plan for marriage is that he uses our differences to teach us how to extend grace and demonstrate it toward each other. Differences can work for your marriage rather than against it if you put in the time to put yourself in your spouse's shoes to better understand them. You can practice this by intentionally making the effort to appreciate your spouse's personality, understand their ideologies, and discuss the expectations

66

that they brought into marriage during the blending process. It doesn't mean that you should think negatively of your own viewpoint and who God created you to be; it just means that you get an opportunity to learn to see things through another set of eyes.

When we were dating, my husband's differences made him the sexiest thing alive to me. His differences stimulated my mind, and I just couldn't get enough of them, but then somewhere within the marriage, we both ended up wanting it our own way. God knew that putting two significantly different people together would create a wonderful unit. It is those differences that help to refine you into an exceptional individual and compliment your life. Those differences make you a triple threat, a "dynamite dynamic duo," and create a unique spice. Over time, our differences became our advantages because when I was weak he was strong, and when he was weak, I was strong. My husband helped me to grow into a more compassionate person and value things in others that I had never paid attention to. Differences may make you feel uncomfortable at times while you adjust and change during your first years; however, God purposed married life for the development of oneness between two people. Remember, you are in the learning phase, so you have to lean on God's grace as you learn. Whatever newlywed process you're walking out right at this moment, know that God has given you the grace to do it well and to do it together, and he is establishing you and building a foundation that will last for the lifetime.

Becoming One by Avoiding the Trap of Comparing

I believe that right now you are writing a great marriage story as a newlywed, and I know firsthand that one of the biggest deterrents to your perfect ending is the personal comparison trap. During the process of becoming one, succumbing to comparison is an easy trap to fall into. There are many opportunities to compare your marriage to those of others. But you must understand that no two marriages are completely alike, and each couple has a different dynamic to and makeup of their marriage. Think about it for a moment. If God made each and every person in the world a certain way, beautifully set apart, special, and unique, how could any couple be exactly the same as any other? The answer is that he did, so we cannot be. Many times, we attempt this perfect ideal of what marriage looks like when the truth is that our marriages will resemble only what you invest in it. When you're investing in something, you are giving special attention to it and pouring yourself and your resources into the investment. When you invest in your spouse, they feel it and know you are paying special attention to them.

Try not believe that your marriage has to look like perfection, thinking that if you are just the perfect spouse, then your marriage will be without any challenges. The beginning of your marriage is the point at which you are in development, so you can't compare chapter 1 of your marriage to chapter 10 or 20 of someone else's. This season represents your beginning chapters, and your beginning chapters involve much development, growth, and togetherness.

Some things in marriage are universal, but each couple has a different mode of operation and different ways that make their relationship tick. Every couple has different dynamic and ultimately cannot be compared to any other couple. Comparing ourselves to others quickly leads us to a place of discontentment. Each husband and each wife has their own strengths and weaknesses, and each couple comes with its own background and unique set of idiosyncrasies. So know that your relationship is creating its own unique flare.

A good example of different dynamics in relationships would be describing how one husband may hate to cook, and another enjoys cooking. Another example could involve one spouse who has had a strong family background and another who comes from a broken home. Some spouses may be quiet and reserved, while others are more outspoken; one wife may be crafty, and another may hate crafts. Your marriage has to come up with its *own unique flavor*. Your flavor may be zesty or spicy or have a dash of cinnamon, but whatever spice it is, it's unique to your taste buds and God's distinct recipe. God opened my eyes about how destructive comparison was within my marriage. I would compare my husband to ideals I had in my head instead of loving the great way he was made. I learned to embrace who he was becoming as a man and as a husband.

Comparisons can happen even if you knew each other very well before marriage, because you still have things to learn as a spouse. So while my husband was learning more about being a husband, I had to change my outlook so I could see him through new eyes. My comparisons made me unable to see his strengths and love him where he was on the journey to who he was becoming. Being a newlywed means being patient while your spouse is still developing and really walking out the vows you spoke and applying them to your life. Marriage teaches you what God's love looks and feels like, and it teaches you how to put into action the words you spoke on your wedding day. There may be some unexpected moments, and unforeseen situations will arise; know that God has given you the grace to walk through them. Prayer is the key to unlocking unconditional love for your new spouse and communicating with God, who created marriage. He will help you handle every situation together as you transition and explore a new life together. The best is yet to come!

Becoming One in the Jewish Culture (Shana Rishona— First Year of Marriage)

The Jewish culture has a time within the first years of marriage called the Shana Rishona, which comes from a passage in the book of Deuteronomy (Deuteronomy 24:5 NLT):

A newly married man must not be drafted into the army or be given any other official responsibilities. He must be free to spend one year at home, bringing happiness to the wife he has married.

When I first heard this, I thought, "Wow, even the Bible addresses the first year of marriage, and the transitions that you undergo!" How comforting it is to realize that even the Lord understands that every newly married couple goes through a time in which they are trying to learn and understand each other within the confines of marriage. Shana Rishona suggests that they should take a whole year just to learn about and become adjusted to each other. They are required to learn to live together before they live with others, so they can be free to devote their attention to the home and each other without the distractions of other people. What powerful imagery of the learning processes and the idea that it takes longer than three to five weeks to become settled within marriage.

Always remember that you are not alone in your transition; couples all over the world, whether they are expressing it or not, are adjusting to life and togetherness. Begin to view the first year as a place of foundation and realize that working on it in the beginning will set a great groundwork for a great marriage. My husband kept telling me in year one, "Give it time, Tamara!" I thought, "How long does this merging take? Shouldn't we have gotten this by now?" He was so settled in his belief that we would eventually get the hang of this and that I needed to be more patient with the process. After year five I realized my husband was right; I needed to be more patient and learn to take things one day at a time.

It's been said that we live in a microwave society, but you don't realize how true that is until you are forced into the slow cooker of love while your marriage dish is being developed. Don't be in a rush but do be excited about the wisdom you are gaining—and by no means does wisdom come quickly. So take things one day at a time, one prayer at a time, in complete surrender to God's plan.

The Bible provides an action plan on what love really is, so we will know how to react when difficulties arise during the process. My newlywed story does not mean your marriage will have the same challenges, but I hope that my sharing my story will help you relate to the process of becoming one and know that you will get through these transitions successfully. If other couples are honest with you, you'll see that most of the feelings you have when adjusting to marriage are normal. The secret is to realize that these transition moments occur as you learn to know your spouse better, come to a deeper understanding of how to operate as part of a unit, and become all that God desires you to be.

It takes the God in you to walk through this phase with a loving, gentle attitude, as he commands. Human nature is naturally selfish, so as a newlywed, you really learn what it looks like to love

God's way. You will feel a tug in your heart like you never have

before, toward loving in one of the deepest ways ever created. It's

the most beautiful transformational experience of your life. Keep

growing and loving year after year, and you will see the wonderful

development of the great marriage that your marriage will be.

The Transition Triangle Δ

(God, New Husband, New Wife)

1. What are you currently learning as a newlywed?

2. In your "becoming one" process, what have you become more aware of with your mate (e.g., being a better listener, putting forth more action, dealing with heart attitudes)?

3. How do you currently prefer your mate before yourself?

4. How would you describe love as a newlywed versus love as a single?

5. Name a way your spouse prefers you and a way you prefer your spouse?

Scripture Meditation

Philippians 2:3 : Do nothing out of selfish ambition or vain conceit. Rather, in humility value others above yourselves,

This scripture focuses on humility, write down how humility helps in relationships.

Prayer

Lord, I thank you for the grace to love in all circumstances. While we are becoming one, Lord, I pray that you will settle within my heart the understanding that becoming one takes time and love, faith, and trust in you. I believe we will not just have an average marriage but a great marriage. A marriage that is intentional and focused on the needs of one another and preferring each other before our own; knowing that I am honoring you in every way.

Lord, I realize that every day is not going to be an easy day, but I thank you that, because you are the center of our marriage, every day we have great hope and expectation that you will be with us through every circumstance. God, be the glue that holds us together and make every day a new day filled with expectation and joy for the journey to together.

In Jesus's name, amen.

CONFIDENTIAL FILE 4
The Newlywed Game

"Two Truths and a Lie"

Now let's play the Newlywed Game! This Newlywed Game was taken from the icebreaker "Two Truths and a Lie" to discuss the facts and fairy tales about newlywed life. I wrote this chapter to address honestly the realities that we face in marriage in a fun and nonconfrontational way.

Let's play!

Statement: Newlyweds are two imperfect people learning to love each other forever.

This statement is true! As a newlywed you are not the perfect person or the perfect spouse, even though we all would like to believe that we are. You are learning to be the best spouse for the one you married, and it's a contract to be a constant learner of love forever. I know we all think we know our spouses fully on day one of marriage, but as we've discussed, it's the journey of marriage that brings about beautiful symmetry, growth, and development. During years one through five, you will learn things that dating didn't teach you, so every day is a new opportunity love better and to grow closer. Commit to loving and learning as the years press forward.

Statement: Being a newlywed is a good time to start new traditions.

A truth! This is the best time to start new traditions and family activities. Begin establishing Christmas traditions, or choose your favorite day for a date night. Maybe it's pillow-talking time; perhaps it's serving the community in a special way. Whatever you decide to implement in your marriage, the first years are the best time to do it, so that your relationship does not get pushed to the side when you take on more responsibilities. Have fun with this!

Statement: Because I married the right one, there should not be any hard days.

Clearly, this is the lie! I thought love needed to be filled with chocolates, balloons, dates, and romantic getaways at least every other day. There was some naivety happening! I quickly found out that after the hard days, my love for my husband grew deeper, and we were able to fight through our differences and still love each other. Beautiful days will be present in your marriage. However, that does not exempt you from days that will be challenging. Yes, even though you married "the one," the depth and beauty of marital love and commitment are found in the better and through the worse.

Statement: It takes some time to develop teamwork.

Truth! I know that teamwork is frequently discussed in premarital classes, and the topic remains valid today and in this book. It takes time to become a team. Remember my telling you how patient my husband was when our differences were laid bare? Well, I was clearly in a rush to feel like a champion in this marriage game. Admittedly, I wanted a championship team without any practice and expected us to flow like the "dream team" from the get-go. I know it's a cliché to say it takes time for teamwork to develop, but understanding

this makes the practice sessions better. What are practice sessions?
These are the moments when you don't see eye to eye or when
your partner doesn't implement what you're asking right away—
when you have to compromise. When you have to extend grace
even though you don't feel like it, when you learn to knock out debt
together...The list goes on and on.

**Statement: Because of my ideas of what a husband or
a wife is supposed to be, my spouse should be what I
imagined immediately.**

Let's get to the bottom of this lie!

Based upon twenty-nine years of preconceptions, I came into
my brand new house with expectations that any husband would
cringe at—and fail! I had written the screenplay of our life and
included many notes on how my new husband's every action, every
good deed, and every romantic gesture would go. It played out like

a big-screen movie. The problem was that I left no room for my husband to become what he was to become. The two of you must remember to take the time to develop into all God desires you to be. Allow your definition of perfection to be rewritten into a perfectly authored work penned by He who is almighty and knows how to do what is best and right and good and perfect for you both.

Statement: Marriage teaches you more about God's love.

Probably the biggest truth of the bunch. Take a look at what God's word says:

Love is patient and kind. Love is not jealous or boastful or proud five or rude. It does not demand its way. It is not irritable, and it keeps no record of being wronged. It does not rejoice about injustice but rejoices whenever the truth wins out. Love never gives up, never loses faith, is always hopeful, and endures through every circumstance.

(1 Corinthians 13:4–8 New Living Translation [NLT])

Wow, what a picture of God's love! You will see now more than ever how much God loves us through your marriage. It's an incredible awareness of love that happens when you walk through the words of scripture, and you feel the depth of God's love as you walk through each life situation. Marriage will push you to love more deeply than you ever have before and challenge you to keep loving with fullness—with everything that you have.

God's love is an unconditional love that is beyond reason and logic; marital love defies logic or reason as well. Marriage causes you to tap into a place where love goes into deep waters. God's love is a deep, deep well, and with his help, we can love through these deep places. Be open to all of the things you're learning about God through your love. If you don't know God, I implore you to accept Jesus's love so you can give love away purely and likewise, receive it. His love never ends, and it is always complete.

Statement: Whatever goals we discussed before getting married, we should achieve quickly.

This is false. We all set goals before marriage that we expect to achieve quickly. So we set huge goals that typically take people years to accomplish and expect for them to be reached within months of marriage. We say things like "I expected that we would live in a bigger house...I anticipated that we would be able to put $4,000 into savings." We want the brand new house, new furniture, and three-figure salaries, and don't forget that we have to take expensive trips in year one of marriage too!

If there's anything I wish I had listened to my parents about, it's taking my time to achieve my goals. It doesn't matter how old you are when you get married, accomplishing the goals you have set for your family will take endurance. Embrace the concept of creating a legacy, and know that, in time and with diligence, it with come forth. In the meantime prepare for, save for, plan for, and dream about the things you and your mate want to do and purchase in the future. Remember, if you have it all in the beginning, then you have nothing to shoot for or be appreciative of.

Statement: Comparing spouses does not help.

Truth.

Don't do it! Don't fall into the comparing-your-spouse trap because what you are comparing your partner to is simply a mirage—something that appears to be real but vanishes because it was only your imagination. When you look at someone else's situation, which may not have your makeup, it's easy for your eyes to compare. Remember, I mentioned in an earlier chapter that your unique married flavor has spices that are specific to your taste. We all don't have the same palate, do we? So water your yard, tend to the lot that you have been given, and let the neighbors admire all the work you have done for the upkeep of your landscape. It's work that only you can do! Comparing takes you into a very unhealthy space and takes up the attention you could be focusing on your marriage.

Statement: Transformation happens as a result of marriage.

Another great truth. Marriage transforms us more into the likeness of Christ. If you don't think so, then go reread the definition of love again and see if it doesn't sound like Jesus. (I hope that by now, you've met him!) When you transform, you allow your character to be molded into the best possible version of who you can be due to Christ's love and light in your life. Marriage is not just something you are getting, or getting into, but something that will get inside of you and transform you in the most beautiful way.

Statement: Having a healthy marriage takes actions with intent.

Listen, great marriages don't fall out of the sky! This statement is surely not just a truth but a piece of wisdom. Newlywed life requires two people who make a decision to love on purpose. Every day that you wake up, you make a decision to love and to do it purposefully. To be truthful my parents made marriage look easy to me, at least from my perspective; however, if I pulled back the layers and the years, I would see the decisions they made to make their love stand the test of time.

I thought my marriage would feel just as simple as I perceived my parent's relationship to be, but all relationships take purposeful actions. Cultivating meaningful connections has indeed become increasingly difficult because the world wants our focus to be external and not focus on what's right in front of us. Do a relationship checkup, and never take your spouse for granted.

Statement: Because you chose me to be your spouse, you should never criticize me.

This is a lie, and a big one at that. I struggled with this thought early in my marriage because somewhere in my mind, I thought that because he had chosen me, there shouldn't be a lot of criticism. Wasn't I indeed perfect for him? Obviously, the person you selected for marriage had to be without flaw since you chose them, right?

Some more naivety for you! That belief system was unhealthy and clearly incorrect. My spouse chose me because he wanted to build a life with me, not because I was perfect in every way. But taking criticism from him required a steep learning curve at first. I often became defensive. I had to learn to take constructive criticism from the person who loved me most, realizing that the more I rejected it, the more I rejected reaching my full potential. So put on your listening ears and listening heart to hear your spouse in those moments; don't turn a deaf ear into a hard heart because it could be the exact conversation you need.

Statement: You're not Jesus or the Holy Spirit!

Truth!

OK, confession time. We all try to be the Holy Spirit's assistant when it comes to the lives of our spouses. Now, there are certainly times when the Holy Spirit will use us as his deputies. However, there are other times when he wants to speak directly to our spouses. We must be mindful of getting out of the way and allowing him the opportunity to do so. There is nothing wrong with expressing your opinion; however, when it comes to the execution of holy expression, it is up to your prayers and the Holy Spirit to get it accomplished. There is nothing that we say that will change our spouses, but the word of the Lord will stand forever.

Statement: Change is not a dirty word.

True. Change has gotten a bad reputation, and it's quite unfair. To recap the definition of *change*, it means to become different; to give a different position, course, or direction; to make a shift from one to another; or to undergo a transformation. I have heard this romantic saying: "The only thing I want to change is your last name." While I love that statement and you should appreciate the fact someone loves you for your personality and who God made you, I also realize change is an inevitable part of marriage. Your whole life must change to make room for your mate. It is how it will work and also how it should be:

Poem:

The day I met you I changed for the better.

There's no place I'd rather be than here with you.

No matter what has come to us, we changed together

I know a love, yes it changed me forever.

Through the years, yes we changed for the better, and then we

grew and grew some more beautifully.

It something to see the way we've changed, I know love, yes it

changed me forever.

Through the years yes, we changed for the better.

Love took us places we never imagined to go,

And if I never met your love, there are things I would never have

seen, yes your love it changed me forever.

And with God before us, who can be against us.

And with God before us we will make it through.

My heart has changed, my mind transformed were walking

hand and hand yes I know a love yes it changed me forever.

The Transition Triangle Δ

(God, New Husband, New Wife)

1. What myth/lie did you bring into marriage, and how have you gained a more balanced viewpoint?
2. What has marriage taught you about God's love?
3. Name real beneficial changes that have happened as a result of marriage and areas in which you have grown as a person.
4. Name changes that you are still adjusting to, and find a scripture to help you in this area.

Scripture meditation: Ecclesiastes 3:1 - There is a time for everything, and a season for every activity under the heavens.

Write down why you think season changes are good our lives?

CONFIDENTIAL FILE 5
Loving without Borders

God uses marriage to perfect you in your love walk by teaching you to love your spouse in all kinds of circumstances. Loving your spouse without borders also teaches you to love others in your life more deeply and purely as well. You will be learning to love another person without many of the conditions we use and set to protect ourselves during the dating phase. We set these barriers to protect ourselves from being hurt and feeling vulnerable while making sure the people we're dating are right for us. But once you're married, you have to give all of yourself without these protective force fields. You're not allowed to run away from challenges that arise, and you have to love on a deeper level.

Before marriage, I had little understanding of how deep my love could go. I never understood how to love a person past the conditions that were in my heart. But my marriage helped me to unravel many layers of love. I've learned to love through life's circumstances, to love under pressure, through joys, tragedy, mountaintops, and valleys. I've taken these lessons and fully know that love is a word full of action that takes on different depths after marriage than it had before. It is a lesson that you are learning, too. Day by day.

Falling in love feels effortless because most things just fall into place at the right time in the right way. Conversely, covenant marriage takes your love to depths that aren't easily explained through a class or a workshop; rather, they are walked out through life. To be honest, I didn't realize my love had borders until I was challenged to love beyond what I felt that I was capable of doing. Love in marriage taught me to believe that love can stand the test of time. I learned this principle through holding on to the promise and covenant I made with my spouse and my God.

Covenant, as defined by scriptures, is a solemn and binding relationship that is meant to last a lifetime. It is important to gain an understanding of covenant before entering into marriage because the climate of our culture challenges the thought that we are supposed to build marriages that last.

Instead, our culture tells us to get out of it! Run away as soon as you experience anything uncomfortable! It is not to be so. We must challenge one another to be countercultural! We have a responsibility as brothers and sisters in the Lord to help one another uphold that which is most sacred and binding to the Master. I am by no means saying that you should stay in relationships where abusive tendencies are consistent and harmful. I am saying that we must not easily shirk the responsibility that has been handed to us for fear of the opinion of others who care not to go the distance. Covenant marriage mandates that we walk this love out until death. Let it be so, and let it be glorious along the way!

The Significance of Marriage

A big question that came to mind when I pondered writing this book was "What is the importance of marriage?" Other than the obvious reason—never having to be alone again in life—why did God create marriage for us to be in, enjoy, and endure? The question helps to settle our hearts on some of the purposes for which God designed for this mysterious love, so let's take a more intimate look at this now.

To begin, God created marriage for companionship, sexual intimacy, and building a family. Another significant reason that he created marriage was to illustrate the possible relationship between God and his creation. I know we would love to think the only reason God created marriage was so we could have fun, have sex, have babies, and live this coveted life of love; however, not being alone is not the only reason God created marriage. When we fully embrace the "why marriage?" question, we can better settle into the purpose of love and marriage, and we won't be so quick to run away during the "for worse" moments. When we connect to the why, it takes us into a purpose deeper than self-fulfillment.

God created marriage for a deeper purpose; it is a symbolic earthly picture of the spiritual relationship between Christ and his bride. The concept of marriage reflects God's heavenly structure on Earth and shows how he had a plan to ensure that we would have access to a relationship with him through Jesus. I will use this opportunity to introduce the ultimate bridegroom, Jesus Christ, who came to Earth as God wrapped in flesh to bring us back into relationship with himself. (How awesome, right?) Ultimately, God created a picture of his enduring love for us; through marriage he desired to show a bond that should never break. There is a prayer of salvation in the back of the book. (Please take a look.) You must know that without the deep abiding love and light of Jesus Christ in your life and marriage, the rest of this book will only be a Band-Aid to a deeper wound. Committing your heart to Jesus Christ is the only salve, the only glue that will hold your marriage together for its greater purpose and greatly expected outcome. Take a moment before you continue reading, and take care of what matters above all things first.

Whether you have had the experience of coming to salvation in Jesus Christ years ago or in the last few moments, you surely know that when you accept Christ, your life changes forever. The life that begins anew with Christ has a significant correlation to marriage and all the changes that take place. I see getting newly married just like the salvation experience of accepting Christ as my Lord and Savior.

How much does your life change after that? In the beginning of your life with Christ, it is the Holy Spirit who draws you to him, and you make a decision to give your heart to him. (A day you never forget.) I will never forget the first day I laid eyes on my husband, because I was blown away when he walked in the room. When our courtship began, it couldn't have been a better moment or better time in my life, and he took my breath away, just like when I encountered the Holy Spirit for the first time. A man then betroths his prospective wife just as the Holy Spirit draws us into a relationship with Christ, and we stand are in awe of all that Jesus is to us. The woman then accepts the proposal to spend the rest of her life with her future husband, just like the day we accepted Jesus as our Lord and Savior. At that point your heart is overtaken with love for the Savior, just like when you get butterflies before dates.

Some people decide to get baptized after they choose Jesus, which is an outward declaration of their love for Christ, and that represents the wedding ceremony, in which you publicly declare your love for each other before witnesses, family, and friends. After the marriage occurs, the wife obtains a new name, and the two become one flesh, just like when we have become with Christ. As followers of Christ, we get new identities, but our new thought patterns haven't quite taken root. It takes maturation and growth to walk entirely as a disciple and follower of Christ. I believe it's the same for marriage. The day you make those vows, there is a unity that happens, but from that point, you being to learn how to walk in your new identity and life as a married person.

Under Attack

The institution of marriage as we know it is under attack due to many not understanding the beautiful purposes of it. Some statistics from the US Census Bureau state that first marriages that end in divorce last seven to eight years on average. This means we need to help other newlyweds through the process of all the new changes they are going through, so their marriages can last. We are growing up in a world that leans toward teaching us to be self-centered and only caring about what's important to ourselves. So many of us are shocked and appalled when our marriages don't look like what everyone posts on Facebook or social networks because we don't internalize the purpose of the vows we just took. Newly engaged couples go to premarital counseling sessions, attempting to come to an understanding of what marriage is but not fully accepting the purposes of marriage in their hearts (head knowledge versus heart knowledge). Magazines, politics, and culture insult marriage because they just do not honestly understand its purpose or actual dynamic, and loving God's way doesn't come naturally. This is why I became so passionate about writing about on this topic; we need to challenge one another to love harder, and say yes to real love. A love that says I love you forever and ever.

Releasing the Border of Conditions and Extending Grace

Conditions begin right from the beginning. By the very nature of the word, dating creates many conditions because we say things like "You must have a good job, a good family, nice appearance, be responsible, know how to dress, be funny..." The list could go on and on. This is the list that we created before meeting our spouses of the conditions they had to meet to be considered dateable. The one that all of our friends tell us to put together so that we can find Mr. or Ms. Right. It's not wrong to have a list—even I had one. But no one tells you about the new list.

After you have chosen "the one," the old list must be quickly forgotten and exchanged for this new list. And this list comes with a word already inscribed across the top, never to be removed, changed, or altered in any way. That word is *grace*. Grace will need to be applied to every part of your relationship, and you will be required to extend compassion, mercy, and patience more than was required of you before you said "I do".. This love is not predicated upon conditions or what the person can do for you. It is based on the foundational words of truth as declared and described by your God.

Now, before you think of what you are not getting, you desire to see them receiving your love without conditions. I had to shift and transition from reacting as if I was in dating mode to responding from a covenant mind-set, as we were now in marriage mode. It's a change that goes from conditional to unconditional and takes you from protection and self-preservation to a complete release of inhibitions and naked transparency.

Life teaches us through failed relationships, hurts, and pains to defend ourselves, to protect ourselves by any means necessary.

Unconditional love tells you to love past those uncomfortable places. Married love looks and feels like the love of God and is entirely different from love experienced outside of the covenant. It's one of the deepest loves you will ever have in your life.

Love Learns to Die to Self

One day I was reading the scripture (I Corinthians 15:36), which says, "When you put a seed into the ground, it doesn't grow into a plant unless it dies first."

For some Godly reason, this scripture gripped me the moment that I read it. I quickly became obsessed with studying the seed and the germination process and comparing them to my processes of growth. This scriptural metaphor is precisely what I experienced in transitioning from singleness to married life because there were so many areas in which I was dying to myself. I found that the key to growing closer to my spouse was understanding that I needed to die to myself. Dying to self did not mean that I was a terrible individual who had treated my husband poorly, but it meant surrendering to the process of transformation. It meant surrendering my will and my single tendencies to execute life now as part of a unit. As a team. Matrimony puts a death to selfishness, and that selfish greed must die for your marriage to feel alive. And just like the passing of that seed, you may feel some pushing, pulling, and cracking and experience some tweaking to get through the outer shell and into the precious jewel inside. That's OK. It's just how it should be. A constant lifting up of grace and surrendering selfishness for the good and perfected end of a marriage that honors the Lord.

So the next time you feel like a piece of your will had to die in your marriage relationship, just imagine the seed and think about how the outer layer of that seed may be dying off, but it's creating roots that are creating a beautiful plant that's budding to the surface. What an awesome testimony of love!

The Border of Fairness in Love

Fairness in marriage is a thought pattern I brought in from my single life. Everything needed to be equal and fair; I definitely couldn't be pulling more of life's load than my husband was! I'll let you in on a little secret. There will be seasons when love is just not fair! These seasons are the part of marriage that people don't always expect. Someone may not always be pulling their weight in a way that you think is balanced.

An example of this would be someone who gets sick and has to do more than the other individual. What if your spouse's job has become more demanding and adjustments have to be made regarding the responsibilities in your household to accommodate their needs? What if someone in your family passes away, and the other person is grieving? What if the other person is trying to lose weight and has to be at the gym longer than they used to be? What if your spouse is going through emotional trauma? God forbid your wife/

husband gets sick and is unable to do the things she/he used to do for a period. Suddenly, you feel a scream rise in your belly and roll off of your lips. "This is not fair! This is not what I bargained for!" Is it fair for you to shoulder the load?

Both my husband and I found ourselves saying this at different points. Whether it was his job that required him to travel, extra demands in our personal lives, or the addition of children to our family. These are the high-pressure moments that we learned about that taught us the realities of moving into a deep sacrificial love. Remember? It is a love that doesn't do things to get things in return; it's a love that tries to do what's best for the unit rather than looking out for itself.

Have you thought about how will you react when situations like these arise? Will you lean toward your single mind-set and say "You know what? I just don't have time for this," or will you press through to what you know is true and right? After a series of fails in this area,

I told myself to stop. I had to stop looking for fairness because real love is not fair. God never said, "If you do this for me, then I will love you"; God never expected for me to be on my best behavior for him to extend his love for me. God's love is so deep that it reaches beyond giving us what we deserve and touches our needs. This is the kind of love you will have to give your spouse in marriage. A love so deep that at moments, it reaches beyond what your spouse deserves and touches their need. When you see something your spouse didn't do, like washing the dishes, calling you to say "I love you" that day, fixing the cabinet you were asking them to mend, or even expressing love in the way you desire to be loved, you then begin to unfold deep love in action. Can you love when it doesn't feel fair?

Loving Past the Border of Offense

Whether you're loving an individual who is not your spouse or you're loving your mate, you will have to learn to love through the offense. There will be plenty of times that your spouse is going to offend you in the beginning while you adjust, and marriage challenges you to learn to keep walking in love through and past those offenses. If your spouse offends you, that doesn't mean that your spouse doesn't love you!

I made this mistake early in my marriage. I took every offense as an attack and convinced myself that if he was attacking me that meant he didn't love me as much as I had thought he did. Can you see how damaging this thought pattern was in the early years? Learning to love past offense is a sign of maturity, and it's certainly not as easy as it may seem. Instead of pretending that it did not offend you, decide to address it. Pray, talk, and make the good decision together not to carry the offense for a long time. Then ultimately, choose to forgive.

Realize that carrying an offense and negative memories too long can make you resentful and bitter. Once bitterness has taken root, it's hard to give love to or receive love from your spouse. Forgive your spouse whether they ask for forgiveness or not, so that your heart will not hold on to things that prevent you from loving the way you should. I always believe that you must have a conversation about whatever hurt you, but you cannot hold on to it. It's amazing how we hold on to things in life, and we don't even realize it. It's important to take inventory of your heart and make sure that you have taken an opportunity to erase the record of your feeling that you may have been wronged.

Prayer Moves Love Beyond Borders

Some might take the role of prayer in marriage lightly, but it is an essential discipline. Often our prayers for our marriages and our spouses help us to adjust, revive, build, grow, and give life to our marriages. None of us has the capability to change our spouses, but God can work on the heart better than we ever could.

There was a time in my marriage when all I could do was pray instead of talk because some discussions would lead to unnecessary argument. I had to let the God who had knit my husband together take control of my situation and my emotions and do work that only he could do. Not only were my prayers effective for him, but they helped me and dug me deeper into God and his purpose for our marriage.

In addition to praying for your spouse, praying together creates an intimate atmosphere that opens your heart to hear the heart of your spouse. I found that in prayer together I was able to hear my husband's heart at times when it felt like communication was not at its best. The foundation of my husband and I's relationship was created through prayer and somehow over the years, the relationship gets clouded with responsibilities and things that need to get done. However, if you meet from time to time in prayer, I promise it's a place of exposure and intimacy. Don't underestimate the power there is in prayer alone and prayer together; they help you connect your heart to hope.

Loving an Imperfect Person

Covenant love means loving a person with flaws, while they are becoming all that they will be. It means being picked to be a part of their growth as a person—God chose you for that. This statement by no means to cosign abusive behavior, but what it does suggest is that loving an imperfect person comes with an extra prescription of grace.

You will have to extend grace to your spouse in many situations within your union. Grace means giving someone something they *do not* deserve. There will be times when you feel like your spouse does not deserve a certain love action from you; however, you will be challenged to love anyway. An example would be treating your spouse in the same offensive way that you saw them behave to prove a point. Loving with the eyes of God—being able to see your spouse as God sees them and allowing God to do the work in your mate—takes practice when all you see is your spouse's imperfections. Do not permit your partner's imperfections to get your focus off the prize, which is having a great marriage! Believe and trust that throughout this journey you and your spouse will learn everything you are supposed to learn to become an amazing couple.

Layers of Love

Layers of love can be paralleled to the rings on the inside of a tree. A tree ring is simply a layer of wood produced during one growing season. So each ring in a tree reflects a year of growth. Newlyweds, this is a great analogy to the journey in marriage, because saying "I do" begins the first layer of your marriage tree.

I remember asking my husband in year three of marriage, "How long is it going to take for us to get it?" Of course, I was looking for easy street, because I am the kind of chick who likes to learn lessons fast and move on to the next thing. My husband, on the other hand, is more of a good-things-take-time person, so we would often have conversations regarding the idea of "Can't we be over this by now?" I know it's cliché to say we live in the generation of *do it now*, but the sad reality is that we do. We want marriages that look like thirty-year- and forty-year-layered trees without going through the seasons that created this fruitful and wonderful looking tree. We also tend to perceive the layer of marriage we are currently in and believe that somehow our marriage will always be in that state, especially if it's not where you want to be.

To find out how old a tree is, you can count the rings inside the trunk. The rings are created by going through the seasons. Each season brings a different temperature and color to the ring; the dark wood that grew at the end of the previous year connects to the lighter-colored part of another tree ring. The lighter color represents quick growth, and the darker-colored part represents the slow growth. The ring could be narrow, meaning there was drought, or it could be wide, which means the tree had abundant rain. Each year, a tree forms new cells, and the annual rings show the amount of wood produced during one season. When I learned this, I thought, "Wow, that's why, when I look at my parents' forty-year marriage, it looks unbreakable. The seasons that they have weathered together—narrow, wide, light, and dark—created a flourishing, beautiful tree that is now not easily cut down. Though you're in your beginning years, know that everything you're learning, good and not so good, is creating a solid tree trunk. Don't be afraid of what each layer will bring; just make sure your tree trunk has its roots dug into Jesus! He gives each marriage tree life, strength, and food through each day.

Love Each Other Deeply

"Above all, love each other deeply because love covers over a multitude of sins" (1 Peter 4:8).

This book was written not only to help you transition into married life but also to give you the challenge to love more deeply than you have before. The scripture written above says, "Above all, love each other deeply." Know that this love will take you into deep waters, but it will teach you so much about life. I had reached a place in my marriage where I wanted more. I didn't just want an OK marriage or a marriage that just coasted through life. I wanted a great marriage!

I wanted a marriage that exuded love on a profound level and in a profound way. Do you know what that means? It means I had to love in ways I had never challenged myself to love before. That love involved me never taking my love for granted, appreciating what he brought to the table, and making a daily effort to show my husband I would walk in love daily.

One of my great mentors told me that saying "I do" is a great statement of love and commitment. Now, walking in love means putting action to those words and proving that love over and over again. When you make the choice to love deeply, to love with purpose, and to love without borders, you will see and experience a level of love that you never imagined possible.

And now? To you!

I am excited about those who are experiencing their new union and the foundations being laid. To those pondering marriage and all that it entails, to those who are engaged and discussing their future together, and even to those who are not-so-newlywed who are encouraged by the word of this book.

I charge you to love through the change, Love through the fun, Love through the beautiful days, Love when you feel like it, and when you don't feel like it. Love NO MATTER WHAT and Love your whole life long.

Now these Newlywed files have been opened, and you have gotten a transparent look into my heart. God has given you all access to love forever and with him as your guide love will never fail. Have fun making memories.

Praying for Your Union and Your Love. Remember...

1. Keep God at the center and foundation of your union.

2. Keep a humble and teachable heart.

3. Don't forget to pray with each other and for each other; your prayers have power.

4. Don't be in a rush, and allow the peace of God to guide your steps.

5. Don't be afraid to ask questions of your trusted mentor.

6. Study your mate's love language and desire to master it.

7. Don't be afraid of change.

8. Prefer your spouse above all others!

9. Make your marriage a priority.

10. Love each other deeply.

Letter to New Husbands

By no means am I an expert on the subject of marriage. Believe me, I am still learning, and this marriage journey is one of lifelong education. However, over the last several years, I've had an opportunity to reflect on my own actions as a husband, many of which are in response to my interactions with my wife, and have come to some conclusions that I think may be helpful in understanding a new husband's marriage license to change.

I would encourage new husbands to enter a marriage with one overarching motivation: to understand that, above all things, the main goal of marriage is a commitment. Marriage vows can be considered very cliché, as we've heard them time and time again, and by the time we say them at our weddings, they just become a regurgitation of what we've heard so many times.

What we must do, men, is truly internalize what we are saying when we say it. We must understand that "for better or for worse" means that, even if the worse outweighs the better, we still are to remain committed. If the sickness outweighs the health, we are still to remain committed.

Finally, this marriage journey is till *death* do us part, and not until dissatisfaction do us part. Gentlemen, I implore you not to enter into your marriage with any sense of entitlement or with the idea that you will have your marriage your way. The marriage experience is wonderful, yes, because you will have many happy moments with your wife, but not only because you will have these wonderful moments, but also because you will grow through the not-so-wonderful moments.

You will experience moments with your wife when you say to yourself, "This is the most satisfying experience of my life," then the next moment say, "This is the most excruciating experience of my life." You'll want her to change her ways to suit your preferences, but what you must remember always is that you chose her. Not only did you choose her, but you chose her as she was when you chose her. You'll find yourself at the edge of sanity if you concern yourself with what your wife could be. Your marriage license was not a certification as a molder of women, but it was a license for you to become the man whom you need to be with the woman whom you aligned yourself with. It is a contract with your bride that says that who you are is who I love and whom I will commit myself to and protect with my heart, my mind, my body, and my resources. She is the one you chose, and she is the one to whom you will remain devoted.

So as you embark upon the journey of a lifetime, always keep in the back of your mind the fact that you have committed to this. You proposed to this woman and changed her life forever. It is now your responsibility to make sure the life you've brought her into is one where she is safe and protected forever. Trust that both your joys and your sacrifices are for the sake of her well-being and that of your future family. You'll reap dividends in your future if you consider yourself the ultimate owner of the destiny of your family, through your dedication to their betterment. But fear not: marriage is not all self-sacrifice. You will find yourself fully satisfied in a mate who is as dedicated to you, or more so, if you create the circumstances conducive to your mate dedicating the fullness of her joy to fulfilling yours.

May God bless you and your family, your marriage, and your future, and keep your eyes steadfast on your mate only. May he bless your offspring, destroy every generational curse that has set its sights on your children, and bring joy, happiness, and fulfillment into your family for generations to come.

In the name of Jesus Christ, the only Son of the only God, amen.

Sincerely and respectfully,

Raymon L. Williams

Letter to New Wives

Hello, new Mrs.! My prayer for you is that you see God's hand in your whole process of learning how to be a great wife. That you see God in your mistakes and that you embrace the idea that God would not have given you something you were not capable of handling. You are equipped for the task, you are equipped for the journey, you can love past walls and love unselfishly, and you can serve as a helpmate to your husband. Always remember God gave you a specific man with specific needs, so study *your* husband, and love *your* husband. You're his distinct rib, and you can help him in a way that no other woman can. You can bring out of him greatness and support him in a way that is purposed for only you. Together, you put ten thousand demons to flight; nothing can stop you two together. Keep your heart close to the Father's as he teaches you and gives you the strength for the journey.

I pray that you experience love in ways that will blow your mind and bring peace and joy to your life. Your husband has found favor now that he has found you, and may that favor pour out to every area of your lives. You are his *good thing,* so never forget that, and may you pursue a great love relentlessly I pray that you pass on and teach other new wives in the future how to sustain their love.

Love,

Tamara

Prayer of Salvation

Heavenly Father, I come to you in the name of your Son, Jesus Christ. You said in your Word that whosoever shall call upon the name of the Lord shall be saved (Romans 10:13). Father, I am calling on Jesus right now. I believe he died on the cross for my sins, that he was raised from the dead on the third day, and he's alive right now. Lord Jesus, I am asking you now, come into my heart. Live your life in me and through me. I repent of my sins and surrender myself totally and completely to you. Heavenly Father, by faith I now confess Jesus Christ as my new Lord, and from this day forward, I dedicate my life to serving him. Amen.

www.ingramcontent.com/pod-product-compliance
Lightning Source LLC
LaVergne TN
LVHW052029080426
835513LV00018B/2239